The Recovery House

The Recovery House

poems

Cynthia Henebry

DEAF SHELL PRESS

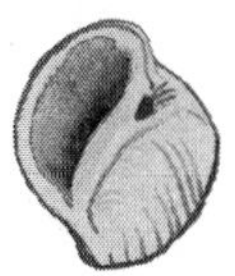

Published by Deaf Shell Press
www.deafshellpress.com

Printed in the United States of America

ISBN: 979-8-9997937-0-6

Cover Image: Cynthia Henebry
Deaf Shell Press logo: Jesse Timmons

for my sons

CONTENTS

II. SHELL

III. WAVE

PROLOGUE

March 1995, Maine

In the woods today,
I tripped on every stone.

I was not a nimble deer
or even a surefooted porcupine,

but I did notice the light
trailing the trees as I went,

heard the pines nudging
each other above,

saw a salmon colored leaf
descend a snowbank,

kept on walking.

I.

FLOWER

DESPITE EVERYTHING

bees on the hydrangea,
gathering heat.

Your own heart
beating, and the sounds

of your ears joining in
with the birds.

Now the lawnmowers!
Don't miss this. Breath

coming in, robin
on the ground,

this
    and this
            and this.

HIBERNATION

I've been mending clothes lately.

File under the category
of things I can control, enjoy,
be in my body while doing.

It's mid-February,
Spring is on its way.
Too soon, for me.

Yellow crocuses are coming up
in Donna and Len's yard.

Heat gathers under my collar,
air thickens in the house.

Non-Negotiable Goals
March 30

do something creative
get in the garden
research mask pattern

THE FURNITURE ANNIVERSARY

I

I celebrated my 17th wedding anniversary
by watching the school board meeting
online, listening to a recorded Zoom
call about white supremacy,

texting my teenage son
about his plans,
and fighting silently
and out loud
with my husband.

Somehow, I am still grateful.

I talked to my 11 year old
about his heart murmur;
brought our neighbor
a meal, self doubted and self
actualized, I even folded
the laundry.

II

Supposedly, this is the furniture anniversary.

Does that mean
I am the furniture, or that we are
bannister, skeleton, stair rail
that allows for something to be
walked through us, onto us, in us
for the next however many years?

There is no resolution
to this, only one
small drop less
self pity.

IN THE LIGHT

I let my face rest
fully—even though I know
it makes me look old.

                                        I am
old—or at least, older

than I've ever
been.

MARCH

The birds
bring back the leaves.

The redbud
Blooms unapologetic—

the pandemic's
second spring.

April 1

make berry muffins
read during the day
pray for my friends

ALL MORNING

the birds have been
trying to wake me, while
the alarm clock sings out
from our younger son's room.

He shuffles out of bed
to mute it, his feet
on the floor like a drum.

Whatever his motivation
for setting it, I can't guess—

A fairy-headed bird careens
toward the window,
lands on the sill,
upside down.

The day begins.

ODE

For Lulu

How I love when your breath
hop skips on the inhale,
the kind that lets
you rest just a little bit more.

Small dog, once called *Tater Tot*
by a first cousin once removed,
whose mother braved rehab
and whose father died
on a mountaintop in North Carolina,
a heart attack at age thirty five.

It's like this, isn't it?
A dog's breath reminds us
of tragedy, resilience-
stars outside at 5:37 am

but I am looking at the screen.
I can hear the sound of the cicadas.
Or is it crickets?
And shouldn't I know this by now?

The train passing through
spurs memory of meditation
in jail.

It is always equal parts sorrow,
equal parts joy.

Elusive for me,
second nature for you.

COMMUNION

There are more cardinals than ever
in the garden this spring.

Tawna says this means the dead
are communicating with us.

Communication with the living
has been difficult these days.

There are more *female* cardinals than ever
in the garden this spring.

I will take what I can get.

April 18

farmers market
family cleaning

cry or sweat

MID-LIFE

for Jenna

At 2 am, my love
snores beside me, sweating
on the sleeping porch where
we have made our bed.

Rain falls. In the distance, cars
pass, owls call back and forth.

Two doors down,
the children are asleep
I hope, especially the older one
whose newly pink hair
frames his olive face,
eyes, nose, mouth.
His determined stubbornness,
that sweetness—
it did not come from us.

I pray I know how to love him.
I pray what we offer is enough.
I pray his life becomes a gift to him
even though we did not give it.

A PRACTICAL GUIDE TO SURVIVING TROUBLED TIMES

Don't take advice from anyone.
Do accept prayers.

If you have a friend, or brother, or cousin,
keep at it until they understand how bad it really is.
They will laugh with you when it's time.

Eventually you'll discover
not getting worse is the new better;
not dying is the new thriving.

Keep fresh flowers
in a vase if possible.
Peonies for perseverance,
sunflowers for stamina.

Don't worry if you're not sleeping.
Good work is happening
in the dark.

Don't take advice from anyone.

Wear yellow or some other color
on your nails, even if
you normally wouldn't.

If you can hear, listen to sounds.
If you can see, look at things.

Touch all of it.

It's okay if it's terrifyingly bad.
Human beings are built to endure.
Remember the people who remind you of that.

Embrace badness, but don't get caught in it.
Watch good TV, whatever that means to you.

If your tragedies have left you
with a functional attention span,
try a little reading as well.
Take walks, if you can.

Lie on your back with your knees
supported and be very, very still.

Don't feel bad if you spend more hours
on your phone than with your family.
Eventually you'll get tired of it.

Don't take advice from anyone.

If at some point you feel consoled
by the fact your life will someday end,

don't
        be alarmed.

This is simply a fact.

In the meantime,
in the meantime,

you are learning
how to live.

April 29

give it all to Wendell

INSTRUCTIONS FOR BEGINNING THE DAY

It is not necessary to take other humans
into your bones. Only
guide them
as you guide yourself,

gently.

Remember sun
is a steady anchor

and although your friend is dying,
she is very much alive.

Like you, like the jays
and finches
and sleeping sons.

Sweep away inadequacy
with your breath.
Be basic.

Begin again

THE NEW RESURRECTION

Staying in bed after the second visit
to the hospital in less than a month,

I made it to the top of the covers,
a wonderful accomplishment
I hadn't noticed before,

when illness was theoretical, imagined,
witnessed, or past. Not present,

as it is in the now
holy moments when I finally understand
my body is the sacred
and primary gift.

Give thanks and praise!

How many times have I
recited that phrase drily,
in the Episcopal
church where I was raised?

Yet these words exactly
are the ones that come—

give thanks and praise!
Again, and again, and again.

May 1

shower
weed the weeds
write a poem
cook something

DRIVING HOME FROM MASS GENERAL

When I become
a cloud again

will I forget
what it was like

to drift
in human form?

Floating past
like that one—

oblivious.
Being its own

reminder,
without even trying.

THE LUCKY ONES

The medical history form asked
if there was any stress in my life
and if so, from what?
LOL.

I answered with precision
and in this order: teenagers,
the pandemic,
climate change.

Brain tumors a distant fourth,
this time.

*

Yesterday at the river,
my dog and I followed a man
teetering on crutches, a full cast
on each of his limbs,
burn marks lapping his face.

When I passed, the words
three cheers escaped my mouth,
by which I meant, holy shit,
you are really doing this.

He smiled a faint comma
then cursed from the pain
of walking
and apologized,
to which I said, *fuck yes.*

*

Farther down the path,
a group of young adults sat
in a circle by the water.
When my dog Layla entered their space,
the delight was palpable.

A man named Moon walked over,
fingernails alternating red, blue, red, blue.
Teeth absent, wide grin.

He complimented my dog's name,
and said they were from
The Recovery House.

May 30

have a good breakfast
stay present on Z o o m

THE WAR RAGES ON

at the bird feeder

  at the hospital

    at home—

another spring day.

BECOMING

Were the spring trees always

this green,
this vivid?

Did I always notice

the light?
(Yes.)

Knowing I will lose birdsong
helps me

to hear it.
These sounds

in my left ear, like church bells
in Belgium. I can almost detect a tune.

Maybe this is what Beethoven heard
when he created *Moonlight Sonata*
as he was becoming deaf.

Not the loss of sound,

the creation
of a new one.

MAGNOLIA

On the way to the family therapist,
none of us breathed.

But at a stoplight,
I saw the magnolia—

leaves curling like tendrils
of new baby hair.

Breathing with us.
Breathing for us,

gentle as air.

June 4

stay awake until it's time to go
to sleep

EARLY SUMMER, PANDEMIC

Two days without a real poem.
My eyes are dry, my stomach hurts,
and the songbirds just keep chattering.

I'm a bad worker.
I'm also a bad housewife.
(What could be more generic than that?)

How can I be dissatisfied
with the quality of my dissatisfaction?
            But I am.

The garden is full of weeds,
the birthday party had too many
cheerful people and the truth is,
I just want to rest.

            In the house,
as neither mother nor wife,
possibilities unfold—

residual rain from a summer storm,
books long neglected,
that article I've been meaning to read.

Or else just wandering
room to room—

that would be enough.

June 28

get the mountains
to my body

BLUE RIDGE

I carried loneliness
to the mountains,
abandoned her there.

The goldenrod did
not mind, the aster
barely noticed.

Imperceptible
she was, waving
in the breeze.

HALFWAY

between this world

and the other,
I panic.

Then a quiet voice says, *welcome*

the silence. Outside the sky

impenetrable blue. Inside

quiet, shimmering,

alive.

July 11

identify wildflowers
from the hike
remember   my friend

ANTIDOTE

Making dinner anyway.

Rooting for the home team.

Sharing the extra protein bar
with the man standing outside in bad weather
whose sign pleads

I am alone.

PRIMAL

Sure I'm scared,
but it's not like I don't
put sunflower seeds in the bird feeder,

make plans with a friend,
take the dog for a walk,
send a poem about not dying

to my friend whose memory
is growing holes.

Take all the time you need.
I'm not going
            anywhere.

August 9

make peach cobbler
celebrate her

THE IOLITE ANNIVERSARY

Twenty one years.
More sober now,

our marriage
can finally drink.

They say it's the brass
anniversary, or iolite—

a mystical stone that stands
for endurance.

We are surely that.

What can I give you
that I haven't already?

I send this question
to the wind-

August 31

pick flowers
tell him *I love you*

DOES IT MAKE YOU FEEL DIFFERENT

he asked, when we talked
about the brain tumors last night.

No, I said firmly.
I already knew.

I hold the warm tea he has made
and remember
we are going to the ocean tomorrow.

For yarrow, nasturtium,
sunflowers and poppies.
For cool June air, wind

that mixes with my breath,
making flowers wave.

I WALK AROUND WITH A BROKEN HEART

I walk across morning wet grass with a broken heart.
I walk to the store and get butter and cream and wine with a broken heart.
I cover June fruit with flour and sugar and a broken heart.
Birds are singing and I can hear them with a broken heart.
Grass grows in the evening sunlight in my broken heart.
The dog's tail wags in my broken heart.
Her pink tongue is a perfect half circle and still
I walk around with a broken heart.
My friends are coming for dinner and I have a broken heart.
There is nowhere it is not, my broken heart.
Blueberry crisp is becoming in the oven-
the table set with a green and yellow flowered cloth-
I walk around with my broken heart.
In my heart, I walk around.

FOR ANNIE

The sun coming out—

such a good reminder,

the sun does come out.

FLOWERS ARE A FORM OF COMMUNICATION

also birds

also rain

when it drops onto your eyelid
while you walk from the car
to the house

your mouth

moving

when you sing a song

the wind

on skin

there is nothing living
that is not communicating

something.

September 8

flowers, shell, sauna, moon

II.

SHELL

OCTOBER

If nothing else, God
is poetic.

            Brain surgery
in my fifty-first year.

In twenty four hours
I lean in
            to the truth:

we don't know,
we don't know.

WIND

in my left ear
like rain before a storm—touching

mastoid, vestibule, cochlea.
Clearing out old sounds

to prepare
for something new.

September 15

wake for the sunrise
prep for sign class
stay o u t s i d e

HARPSWELL

I drove eighteen hours to sit

on the dock of our rental cottage,
feet plunked into water.

Will I be deaf by this time next year?

The arctic tern
swans overhead.

Either way, the water
keeps shifting.

MY MOTHER

nursed her heartbreak
on the couch where I nurse mine.

No longer here, her sympathy
rises from the cushions. A hint

of *I told you so* but mainly,
            Sorry.

I'm sorry, I'm sorry.

SOUNDS BOUNCE

around the stratosphere
of my mind.

No, brain—one sixth of it   space
uncharted,
                    unknown.

An astronaut in my own galaxy,

ground control
unnecessary.

Move in, not out.
In, not out.

          In, in, in.

With every word, gesture,
request, command:

          in, in, in.

Let nothing that moves
out not be connected
to this—

HELENE

Three days before brain surgery,
the sound of rain
in my left ear

for the last time.

I can't process this
so the poem rushes in,
saving me from trying.

Though it has destroyed
houses, roads, lives
in the southern states,

the rain says
shush, shush—

I'll find other ways
of speaking with you.

September 23

go slow
plant fall greens
deadhead the cosmos

THE AUDIOLOGY BOOTH

Say the word *baseball.*

Say the word *cowboy.*

Say the word *sidewalk.*

Say the word *ice cream*

Say the word *ear drum*

Say the word

Say the word *mousetrap?*

Say the word *sky scape?*

Say the words *bad ear*

No.

Say the words *struggling to hear*

No.

Say the words *let go*

Say the words *all done*

Say the words

after thirty years, I don't have to listen to his orders anymore.

A surprising and silent relief.

ONLY SILENCE

I lost all the hearing in my left ear yesterday.
All of the hearing is gone. The hearing disappeared.
There are no more sounds coming in.
The ear doesn't hear anymore. I am deaf
in the left ear, and nearly so in the right.
The ear has become deaf. Only silence—
a vacuum in the left ear now.
Yesterday, the hearing in my ear took a long hike
off a short pier. I can't hear sounds with my ear anymore.
Only pressure and buzzing in my ear now.
So why does it keep coming back to "I have lost"?
There is no more hearing in the ear.
Lost: sounds, music, easy conversation.
Birds (that one with a sad gasp),
our sons' voices; dog's snoring.

But this knowing, that god put me here.
And people look at me directly
when they talk now, their mouths a
portal to my heart.

October 2

exercise
stay out of my head

ON THE DAY AFTER I BECAME MORE DEAF

the beach was littered with them—
opaline shells, the size
of a half dollar, the width of a pick.

They look like ears, I thought,
and placed them on top
of my own.

If an ear doesn't receive sound,
what can it become?

An instrument of beauty
and awe? I wonder,

will I still hear the sound of the ocean
if I place a conch shell there?
Or is what that childhood game revealed
endlessly apparent now?

Oceans without, within.

IT'S FOGGY THE MORNING I LOSE MY HEARING

Not so much *lose*, but be released
of it,

have it carved from me,
a pearl from an oyster.

(Always with the ocean metaphors
these days).

I decide to stop holding my left ear
closed
to see what it will be like.

It's like this right now.

Fall back, receive, now
it's yours for the taking.

Who says I can't gift the birdsong
when I lose it?

THE FOURTH TRAUMA RESPONSE

Once noticed, the fawn
wanders away—not running

  or rushing, but heading
back into the world

    curiously

wet nose grazing
late summer flowers,

    kissing

the ground
  she walks on.

October 14

rest when I remember to

AT DAWN

on the morning
of your 49th year

you fold your body
into mine. Birdsong

then a parade—
fire trucks roaring.

Your scent rises up.

PACKING LIST FOR BOULDER

- pesto
- his favorite vintage t-shirts
- camera
- meds and chargers
- hiking boots
- therapeutic apology

LABCORP

In the waiting room,
the chairs are full
with those of us who
will share our blood
with hopes of something
being discovered or not.

An almost love affair
has grown between two
patients, so when he goes
back with the nurse,
her leg starts anxiously tapping.

"Sweetie," he says with a smile,
"I'll see you again soon."

And he does,
but only for a minute
before leaving
the facility for good.
Her leg starts up again.

November 1

clean the office
walk and stretch
stay out of bed

ODE TO SNORING

Birdsong pours in
through open windows,
sparkling like stars.

I forgive
my husband
for his middle-aged body

and remember
something
in the act of it.

The sun cleanses me.
Roughly at first
then gently—

outstretched arms
towards every open cranny.
I will forgive

this world
into being, beginning
with myself.

THE OUTPATIENT PAVILION

My people. Those with canes,
wheelchairs, visible scars.

Those in gowns and socks
like they're heading to a sleepover.

A mother holding her daughter's small hand.
The tender nurse who draws my blood.

A janitor pushing trinket gifts on a trolley.
The couple who slow down to tell a woman
she is dragging her coat.

Vulnerability is on display here
and thank god

because now I'm in the audio booth,
listening for the tones

and they are slowly

slipping

a w a y

PRESENT SOUND MEMORY

What even is

the memory of a sound?

Not possible to name

in the now

holy

moments

this new

silence brings.

A new world

unfolds,

if

I let it—

November 9

stack firewood
light candles

THINGS THAT SEEM LIKE A POEM

Flowers falling
from the sky.

Recovering my son's phone
from the police.

Getting splinters.
Leaving them in.

YESTERDAY

my son took some clothes
from Walmart without paying.

Because I wanted them and didn't
have the money, he said.

The black employee offered
my white son grace.
No consequence, *this time.*

Now, it is we
who issue the punishment:
love's wise boundary of *no*
you cannot have everything.

When my son was a baby,
he needed to be swaddled
extra tight. We'd cinch it

and cinch it and only when we
thought he couldn't breathe,
did his body finally start to relax.

COMPLETE SILENCE

on the morning drive.

I could feel him glancing
at me, simmering—

I was peaceful if only
for lack of sleep.

Nothing more needed to be said.

Last night's declaration of
you don't understand me

ringing invisibly
between us.

A NEW LOW

My son suspended—

not from gossamer threads
like the spider in our yard
whose geometrical web
is a wonder—

from school

for writing
on the bathroom
walls

and

I don't know where
this poem goes next.

PONY PASTURE

After we confronted our son
about his drug habit
I went for a walk

found a small feather
with black and blue stripes.

I carried it home, carefully.

He had already
fallen asleep,

I placed
the small feather
on the phone
by his head,

sweet brown curls
covering
his innocent face.

November 18

savor his sweetness
ice-cream cake

FALSE SECURITY

Last night you asked if we could move
at least once before you leave home.

You want to know what to expect,

your nine year old self sensing
the stability we provided
is too much of a crutch.

I can't draw a map
of all my childhood homes,
too many to count, and my attachment
to each growing dimmer—

After the fourth one,
my mother asked,
aren't you sad to be leaving?

I didn't know what to say.

I did mark the second one—
my name on the wall, a small
act of rebellion, my nine year old self

saying, *here, here.*

November 23

hike
dance
paint

LEARNING TO LISTEN WHILE THERE'S STILL TIME

for Katya

If you want to know

what

noise

the cardinal

makes just watch!

Her orange beak expands

and the Universe

is filled—

every sound

a sacred

Word.

IMAGINE

Imagine a painting of a heart.
Imagine a painting of a heart
with your face pressed on it.

Imagine a painting of a heart
and two trees—
                    no, a forest.

Imagine a painting of the moon,
nearly full.

Imagine a painting of the group home
with bored but secretly hopeful teenagers
on the worn and cozy couch.

Imagine a painting of the fireplace
next to a Christmas tree, the cat
and dog warming themselves by it

and everything that happened this year
and everything that will happen next.

Imagine a painting of the Red Sox game
in 1999. It was raining, or was it sunny?

Imagine a painting of the two of us,

falling in love like how we are
falling in love now—still, tender

          in older bodies.

FUTURE SOUND

after Khalil Gibran

How can I know the loss
of the cicadas until I feel it?

The tinny symphony
lights up my left ear.

My heart aches with not knowing,
the anticipation of grief.

A symptom of
life's longing
for itself
Gibran said.

On the right, crickets—
in a manner of speaking, that is.

WHAT IF JOY

What if joy
what if joy

is the sound

what if joy
is the sound

my new ears make

what if joy
is the sound
my new ears make

when no-one else is
watching?

THE LAST PLAYLIST

There is only this moment,
and what we have left behind.

Whistling.
Songbirds. The sound

of your voice, and mine.
Our lives together, dancing—

more full of song
than ever before.

PACKING LIST FOR HOSPITAL

- coconut water
- bananas
- grey journal and pencil
- chargers, brush, dop kit and toothbrush
- face lotion
- knitting (the bag with Annie's blanket)
- pink eye pillow (very important)
- underwear
- rainbow sweatpants
- shells
- me!

November 29

b r e a t h e

REFLECTIONS

My new face,
fallen.

A flower,
resting

on a shell.

HOW

How do I listen to rain for the last time?

Like I am listening to it
for the first time.

This is not a fancy exercise,
no need to go deep.

It slips away as
I pay attention.

A car drives down the street,
splashing through a puddle.

My heart breaks, opens.

WITHOUT SOUND

I can finally see the birds

the birds.

III.

WAVE

CHRONIC

Good news always comes with caveats,
you said, letting me know
you understand my reaction
to the results.

Like the Zen saying *life*
is like stepping into a boat
that is about to sail out to sea
and sink.

But oh, before then!
The waves, the sun, the wind
and rain.

If it's not my fault,
then what's happening to me
is a very big adventure.

December 1

write a letter
order yarn

IN THE BEGINNING

for Pat

You were the shell—

protective, receptive. Opening

to the Universe as

life as it is poured in.

*

Every kind of weather transformed you.

In the distant future, shell

becomes ocean becomes sand.

*

We ride waves

together, unending—

THE FIRST HIKE

Breathe in wet

pine needles

roots

rocks

stones

tripedal

with my cane

no walking stick

no cane

salty air cormorant sky

ground

hello

WAVES

I can breathe
underwater

now, nothing

to fear but
swimming out—

open waters
of sadness,

relieve my lungs
of their weight.

December 16

s t a r s

AFTER YEARS

it becomes easier
to see the love in it.

Falling asleep
on a snoring dog,

a cup of warm tea
between us.

Even our son, drunk
on Christmas morning,

beloved cat
gone missing.

My heart cracks,
opens—

alternatives
far worse.

WINTER'S SPARENESS

Thin limbs between me
and a pinking sky.

December 21

be quiet

THE FIRST TIME I MET YOU

I was atomized—

shimmering
    reduced

to small particles   I am

the first course correction

your anger
    at all the men's voices

on my answering machine.

Twenty six years later,
    the second one.

You

remind me there are
    other women

in this Universe.
I dissolve

    in understanding

you're not
    the only man.

THE PORCELAIN ANNIVERSARY

Remember
when we were porcelain?

We're not now.
We're not.

I ONLY HAVE TO REMEMBER

The seasons' passing is the main event.

Gathering snow around stalky seed pods.

The whine of a garbage truck.

The train whistle bellowing. Right now,

the Universe so vast—no wonder

I carry small pieces back home.

This longleaf pine bough,

my grandmother's vase. Even these bones

under and over. I own none of it, and yet—

December 28

be still

FAMILY DINNER

On an undetermined day
in the very near
future,

he will move out.

Still, I light the candle.
Still, I set the table.

Tonight
his hand is warm

I hold it.

HIS FATHER'S MOVING OUT

Where will you go? he asks.

Where have you gone? I think.

Does

the maple

lose her leaves

or does she choose

to let go

with a

sigh?

NOW GRIEF COMES

The absence of my son's voice,
an Irish accent, the source
of the joke. The sound

of leaves
falling from trees.

Since the surgery
only half my face cries,
the other side refuses
            the sound

of my voice,
calling our dog's name.

I just burned my first bowl
of deaf popcorn,

                        but barely.

December 31

let go

OF TEARS

holding

your hand

on the

verge all

the way

around the

pond.

NEW YEAR'S DAY

Trees bounce
as I take steps
towards the lake
of last night's conversation.

I fill the bird feeder,
gather kindling
by the door.

The urgency
before the end
of the year
to tell everyone
you love
that you love them
has passed. Now

we stare blankly
back and forth
under a white sky.

THE OCEAN

There is a way in which   the sick
are on one side of things,   the healthy
on the other.

I don't mean like war
but perhaps an island

and the water
that surrounds it.

You, on land.
We, out here,

riding waves, taking in
the sun, rain, wind,

and the moon—
lapping at your shores.

WAYS TO LISTEN TO THE SNOW

The black cat is curled on the
blanket you knitted
during the pandemic. His belly rises
and falls.

The scar on your face reflected in
the computer screen
is red, but healing.

A fine white dust covers the grass
that surrounds
The clay pots on the patio.

Water pools on the school's
parking lot.
You breathe, the cat breathes.

Outside, the snow falls and falls—
a kind of breath itself.

January 2

night   sky

WAYS TO LISTEN TO OTHER HUMANS

Notice the sound of your breath.

Make breakfast.
Have a second cup of tea. Sit down

on the bluish grey family couch.
Let go of the idea that you want him
to talk.

        See if he talks anyway.
Keep not talking.

Pay attention
        to yourself.

THE SEASON HASN'T CHANGED, HE HAS

The plants were never melancholy

at the thought of leaves dropping.

In fact, they were celebrating—

falling orange, yellow, purple, red,

giving all they've got

as if this were the last time they could shine.

JANUARY

On the way to the airport,
I remember myself.

        Now, he is in touch
        with his inner life?

Now I am innerly quaking.
Not really though, not really.

        Just a small tremor,
        just a slight shake.

Just a small reminder
of being bone and dust,

powdered snow
on the sidewalk

as we drive by in Boston.

January 13

set a pretty table
light the fire

UNDEFENDED HEART

Tell him

you love him even though

he's moving out.

Know in your bones

you give

nothing

away

in the act.

RAINBOW CLOUDS

shells,   I'd never seen before

  sky

the sea

          rainbow

clouds,

shells,   I'd never seen

          sea   clouds

shells   sky

          sea.

February 1

write down my dreams

BACK AT THE HOSPITAL

Am I losing my emergency contact?

He's napping in the chair beside
my gurney.

He doesn't want to be here,
but he is.

I reject thinking in absolutes,
return attention to my belly.

I'll let him take
the blue teapot with the green
knitted cozy I brought
back from Ireland.

BEFORE WE SAY GOODBYE

I remove a splinter
from his thumb, rinse
the tweezers in the sink.

Outside, the birdfeeder he gifted
two Christmases ago, overfull

with birds: cardinal, purple finch,
chickadee, all come to watch
as tears pour from my eyes.

I set grief aside, open
to sadness.

We step into the unknown
together. Now also, apart.

February 14

Deaf dance party

MORNING RITUAL

Our fingers touch when
you hand me the warmish tea

a complete circle.

FIRST NIGHT

They're not here.
My family has left.
Tonight, the boys will sleep
at their father's house.

When I met my husband,
he was a boy,

    we fell in love—

Twenty six years
of anniversaries, surgeries,

            flowers, shells, waves

wash up on the shore of
            this moment.

I cast about
            for a stone, finding no one

to throw it at.

Tiny

half

moon

holding

up

the

sky

March 1

grieve
be joyful
pour the tea

The redbud blossoms are in the future again.

NOTES

The idea for *Non Negotiable Goals* came from a series of daily texts with Gayle Maslow that began during the 2020 pandemic.

Future Sound. The line "life's longing for itself" is from the poem "On Children" by Kahlil Gibran, which can be found in his book *The Prophet* (Knopf, 1923).

> *Your children are not your children.*
> *They are the sons and daughters of Life's longing for itself.*
> *They come through you but not from you.*
> *And though they are with you yet they belong not to you.*

Chronic: "Life is like stepping into a boat that is about to sail out to sea and sink" is attributed to Shunryu Suzuki Roshi in Pema Chodron's book, *Living Beautifully: With Uncertainty and Change* (Shambhala, 2012).

When I First Met You is a poem in response to one that Andrew Schoeneman wrote and recorded for my hearing ears, just before the last brain surgery. That poem is called *The First Time.*

> *Love pours out, amounts so*
> *Perfectly proportioned*
> *To need*
>
> *They are finally endless*

ACKNOWLEDGMENTS

Thank you to the Redbud. Thank you to the Styrax, the Serviceberry, the Poppy. Thank you to the Birds. Thank you to the men in my life. I learn from being in relationship with you every single day. Thank you to the women who continue to shepherd my life, and supported this collection into being: you know who you are. Thank you Spring Brook Sangha, the Fellowship Foundation, and The Blue Shore Poets. Finally, this collection would not be in your hands without the love, magic, and skill of the poets and editors Heather Mackay Young and Holly Wren Spaulding. To all of you, a deep and grateful bow.

ABOUT THE AUTHOR

Cynthia Henebry is a poet and photographer. She is a graduate of The Academy for 5 Element Acupuncture and Virginia Commonwealth University's School of the Arts. Her photography has been exhibited at the Virginia Museum of Fine Arts, the National Portrait Gallery, and other museums and galleries throughout the United States. She lives with her family in Richmond, Virginia, where she was born.

The Recovery House is typset in Garamond Premier Pro.
Book design by Lindsay Lake.
Composition by Bookmobile Design & Digital
Publisher Services, Minneapolis, Minnesota.
Manufactured by Bookmobile on acid-free,
100 percent postconsumer waste paper.